The Riley Press and
Shahin Stone
present

The Low Cost
Index Funds Guide

Author: Shahin Stone
Editor William J. Riley
Published by The Riley Press, a wholly owned subsidiary of Trikke.MI
Pleasant Ridge, Michigan
Evanston, Illinois

Table of Contents

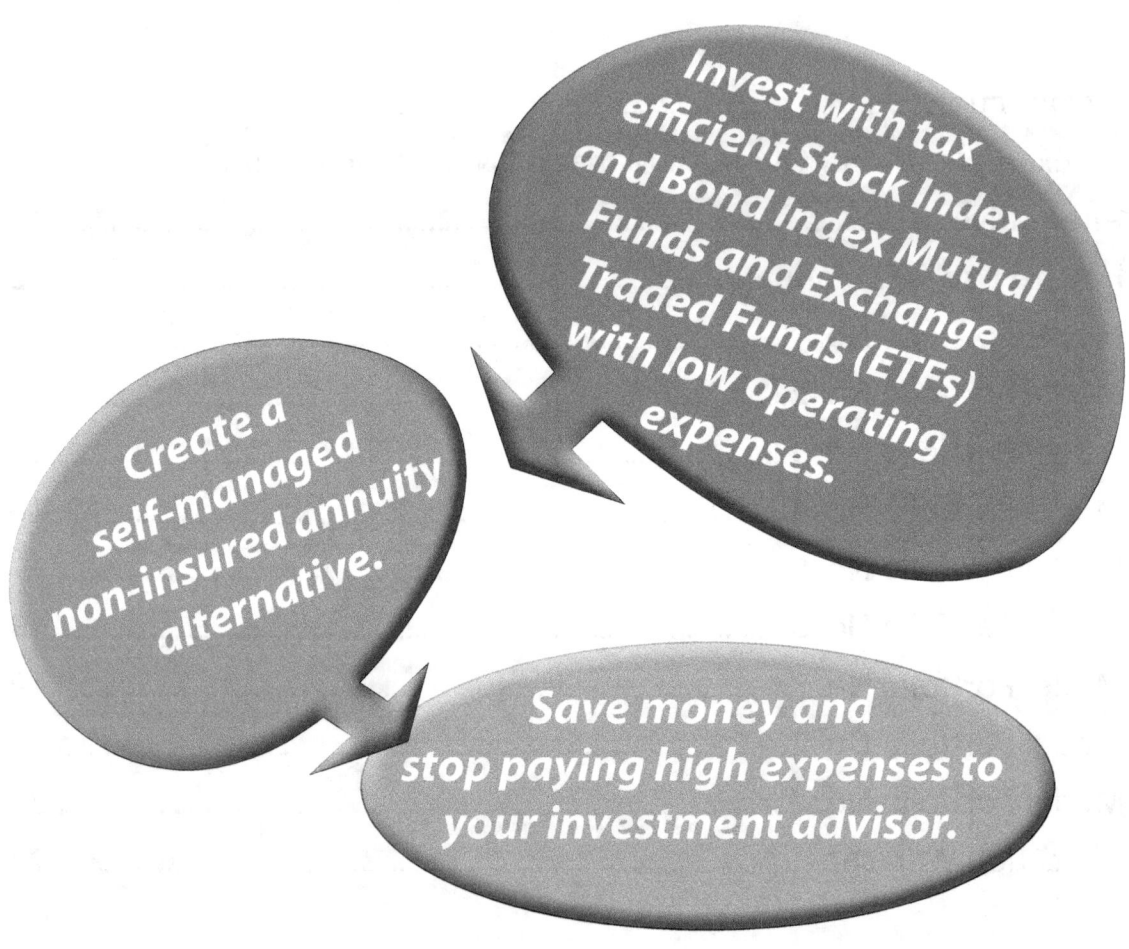

Introduction

Do you want to invest in the stock market? You could listen to all the business channels and subscribe to all the financial newspapers and magazines and then try to select your 8-10 stocks for your portfolio; OR you could invest in low cost index funds that historically do better than 80-90% of expensive actively managed funds.

No more wasted money and time on financial newspapers, magazines and business channels.

Simple and smart.

Introduction

You can create an Annuity Alternative with minimum risk and no danger of losing your principal upon death. Inflation can diminish the value of your guaranteed income from an Annuity.

As with all non-insured investments you could lose some or all of your principal investment and there are no guarantees of future performance.

Always consult with your Financial Planner, Attorney and Accountant regarding investments and tax consequences.

Embrace an Annuity alternative without giving your lump sum principal to an Insurance Company.

- Very low operating expenses
- Unlimited withdrawals without penalty
- Easy access to your money for emergency expenses
- No Insurance Company involvement
- Allocation recommendations with percentages based on three degrees of risk tolerance along with worksheets
- No gimmicks or Market Timing nonsense
- No loss of principal balance as a result of death
- Nine Model Portfolios that are designed for this Annuity Alternative **and all regular and retirement investment plans**

There is nothing like creating a plan and sticking to it.

- Maximum flexibility
- Diversification

You need to be in the Market on its best days for maximum results

- **This guide is not just for Baby Boomers and is the best money you will ever spend. This is the simple and smart way of investing!**

When a Chief Financial Officer of a leading Ivy League University Endowment says that there may be only two or three Asset Managers in the country he would consider using and that **Tax Efficient, Low Operating Cost Stock and Bond Index Funds** are the best way to invest; one should pay close attention. We believe that you will agree!

This information is designed for and will benefit regular and retirement investment plans.

If an investment existed that could legitimately promise great returns with little or no downside risk the chances are it involves elements that will not stand the test of time or the exposure to broad daylight. Flipping houses is a popular get rich quick scheme that claims to operate on someone else's dollar. I imagine there is a house somewhere that can be bought for a few hundred dollars but it likely will require major sweat equity or some miracle of fate to turn from a loser to a winner. Why would someone tell others about such a magic money machine? Selling seminars on getting rich is the current incarnation of the Carnival Con Games of yore.

Explore the Self Managed Annuity Alternative.

Remember that inflation can eat away the value of your guaranteed income from a typical Annuity.

Take control of your financial future and stop paying excessive fees and operating expenses.

Questions – Statements you need to read and understand before choosing any Savings, Retirement or Investment method.

Saving for retirement while paying high fees and commissions for investments with high maintenance costs is like trying to wash in a sink without a stopper. You will dump a lot down the drain to no use.

We want you to invest in products with low maintenance fees. How do you know what a low maintenance fee looks like? It is typically less than 0.50 %, often 0.25% or less.

Aggressive investing is expected to return a higher return than conservative investing. There is a middle ground for those who do not feel particularly conservative or aggressive. The moderate road will usually mix Bond Funds with Stock Funds and will likely include Index Funds. Index Funds will tend to track the Market as a whole for the sector that they target.

Some companies have better track records than others but prudence is the best guide. If a return looks too good then ask yourself why the proponent would tell you or anyone else about such a perfect investment. Did the original investors in Apple know something or were they in the right place at the right time and had the courage to take a risk?

What a Single Premium Insurance Company Immediate Payout Annuity looks like:

$100,000 Lump Sum Immediate Payment for Life

For Male, age 65, $567 per month or $6,804 per year.

Annual yield is 6.8% but this is done by returning some of your principal as long as you live.

You cannot undo this purchase.

The payments terminate upon death of the Annuitant and Heirs receive nothing.

If you do your own Annuity you could receive annual payments of $6,804 assuming zero growth for 14.7 years and any residual balance would go to your heirs and not be lost upon death.

Investment Advisors are typically overrated.

If they manage a Billion Dollars for a 1% fee they will take $10,000,000 (**yes, that is TEN MILLION DOLLARS**).

Imagine managing 10 Billion Dollars – that 1% fee becomes **ONE HUNDRED MILLION DOLLARS. And that doesn't include money made from 12(b)(1) marketing expenses and commissions from your portfolio turnover.**

If you invest in 4 stocks from 10 sectors you have a 40 stock portfolio. Instead of billing you for a percent of assets under management they should charge a reasonable flat fee.

You can negotiate flat rates for Real Estate Brokers and selling a $200,000 home takes about the same effort that selling a $100,000 home takes.

Your Stock Broker doesn't control the market and history shows that being in the market on all days is better than entering and leaving (Market Timing) unless you believe in luck and magic.

Fees should be based on a reasonable percentage and the most reasonable fees are those charged by Index Funds.

An Example of Your Own Self Managed Non-Insured Annuity Alternative

$100,000 Lump Sum Investment

Figured at zero principal growth which is possible but unlikely. Imagine what it would be 2%, 5%, 7% or higher.

$100,000 Lump Sum. Immediate Payout at end of each year.

Male

At Age	Annual Withdrawal	Monthly Withdrawal	If zero growth, Principal lasts for
55	$5,676	$473	17.6 years
60	$6,384	$532	15.7 years
65	$7,152	$596	14 years
70	$8,148	$679	12.2 years
75	$9,648	$804	10.4 years
80	$11,844	$987	8.4 years

Female

At Age	Annual Withdrawal	Monthly Withdrawal	If zero growth, Principal lasts for
55	$5,256	$438	19 years
60	$5,796	$483	17.2 years
65	$6,528	$544	15.3 years
70	$7,248	$604	13.8 years
75	$8,640	$720	11.6 years
80	$10,704	$892	9.3 years

In the first section you learned a little about why you should manage your own money. In the following sections you will find specific advice on where to invest your money and how much of it should be in the various choices.

Begin by deciding how conservative or aggressive you want to be. This is often a function of how long you have before starting to draw on your retirement program but other factors should be taken into account such as other resources that can provide a safety net. If you are not sure which range to use then consider your response to the following statements:

- I never buy a lottery ticket! *You are probably very conservative.*

- I may buy a lottery ticket when the pot gets really big or I feel especially lucky! *You are probably moderately conservative.*

- I buy lottery tickets on a regular basis! *You are a bit aggressive.*

You should adjust for your other resources such as Social Security benefits, the life style you want to achieve and any other factors that would affect the amount you need for retirement and the time available. Conservative approaches opt for security over growth and therefore present a lower final amount. Aggressive approaches risk more for the chance at a greater return. A basic tenet of investing is to keep the majority of your principal safe but invest in some risky areas for the Golden Ring.

The second decision to make is the age at which you would like to start your funded retirement. Remember that you may be augmented by Social Security or other payments.

The third decision is how much you want to receive on a monthly or annual basis.

With those decisions (the answers are not permanent and you should revisit these whenever life events arise that can affect your retirement) you begin by looking at all nine of the Model Portfolios in order to achieve your financial goals.

Model Portfolio 2 uses Bond and Stock Index Funds from Vanguard.

Remember that in basic terms, Bonds are Conservative and Stocks are Aggressive. Using Bond Index Funds limits the risk of losing Principal.

Model Portfolio 1 is more Aggressive using Stock Index Funds more so than Model Portfolio 2.

Model Portfolios 3 through 9 follow the same investment guidelines but use other Companies. Some people prefer working with one company over another. The listed companies have a track record of giving the Investor good products.

Next, you use the Allocation Worksheet to pick percentages to apply to the chosen Model Portfolio and you will have your Own Private Annuity and your Individual Regular and Retirement plans.

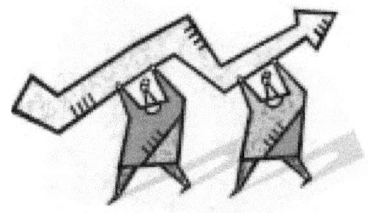

Model Portfolio No. 1

With Vanguard Stock Index Funds

Item	Alloc.	Stock Index Fund	Symbol	Op.Exp. Ratio
1	40%	Vanguard 500 Index Fund		
		Admiral Shares	VFIAX	0.05%
		Investor Shares	VFINX	0.17%
2	15%	Vanguard MidCap Index Fund		
		Admiral Shares	VIMAX	0.09%
		Investor Shares	VIMSX	0.24%
3	15%	Vanguard SmallCap Index Fund		
		Admiral Shares	VSMAX	0.09%
		Investor Shares	VAESX	0.24%
4	30%	Vanguard Total International Stock Index Fund		
		Admiral Shares	VTIAX	0.14%
		Investor Shares	VGTSX	0.22%

Information Only

Vanguard Prime Money Market Fund VMMXX Op. Exp. Ratio 0.17%

With Vanguard Stock Index Funds (60%) and Bond Index Funds (40%)

Item	Alloc.	Stock Index Fund	Symbol	Op.Exp. Ratio
1	20%	Vanguard 500 Index Fund		
		Admiral Shares	VFIAX	0.05%
		Investor Shares	VFINX	0.17%
2	10%	Vanguard MidCap Index Fund		
		Admiral Shares	VIMAX	0.09%
		Investor Shares	VIMSX	0.24%
3	10%	Vanguard SmallCap Index Fund		
		Admiral Shares	VSMAX	0.09%
		Investor Shares	VAESX	0.24%
4	20%	Vanguard Total International Stock Index Fund		
		Admiral Shares	VTIAX	0.14%
		Investor Shares	VGTSX	0.22%
5	10%	Vanguard Total Bond Market Index Fund Investor Shares	VBMFX	0.20%
6	10%	Vanguard Long Term Bond Index Fund Investor Shares	VBLTX	0.20%
7	10%	Vanguard Intermediate Term Bond Index Fund Investor Shares	VBIIX	0.20%
8	10%	Vanguard Short Term Bond Index Fund Investor Shares	VBISX	0.20%

Information Only

Vanguard Prime Money Market Fund VMMXX Op. Exp. Ratio 0.17%

With Fidelity Stock Index Funds

Item	Alloc.	Stock Index Fund	Symbol	Op.Exp. Ratio
1	60%	Fidelity Spartan 500 Index Fund		
		Investor Shares	FUSEX	0.10%
		Advantage Shares	FUSVX	0.06%
		Institutional Shares	FXSIX	0.05%
2	40%	Fidelity Spartan International Index Fund		
		Advantage Shares	FSIVX	0.12%
		Investor Shares	FSIIX	0.20%

With Fidelity Stock Index and Bond Index Funds

Item	Alloc.	Fund	Symbol	Op.Exp. Ratio
1	%	Fidelity Spartan 500 Index Fund		
		Investor Shares	FUSEX	0.10%
		Advantage Shares	FUSVX	0.06%
		Institutional Shares	FXSIX	0.05%
2	%	Fidelity Spartan International Index Fund		
		Advantage Shares	FSIVX	0.12%
		Investor Shares	FSIIX	0.20%
3	%	Fidelity Spartan U.S. Bond Index Fund		
		Investor Class	FBIDX	0.22%
		Advantage Class	FSITX	0.10%

With Schwab Stock Index Funds

Item	Alloc.	Stock Index Fund	Symbol	Op.Exp. Ratio
1	%	Schwab S&P 500 Index Fund	SWPPX	0.09%
2	%	Schwab S&P 1000 Index Fund	SNXFX	0.30%
3	%	Schwab Total Stock Market Index Fund	SWTSX	0.09%
4	%	Schwab International Index Fund	SWISX	0.19%
		For information only		
5, 6	% %	For Schwab Small Cap Index (SCHA) and Schwab Mid Cap (SCHM) Index Funds, Schwab offers Exchange Traded Funds (ETFs)		

With Schwab Stock Index Funds and Schwab Bond Index Funds

Item	Alloc.	Schwab Stock Index Funds	Symbol	Op.Exp. Ratio
1	%	Schwab S&P 500 Index Fund	SWPPX	0.09%
2	%	Schwab S&P 1000 Index Fund	SNXFX	0.30%
3	%	Schwab Total Stock Market Index Fund	SWTSX	0.09%
4	%	Schwab International Index Fund	SWISX	0.19%
		For information only		
5, 6	% %	For Schwab Small Cap Index (SCHA) and Schwab Mid Cap (SCHM) Index Funds, Schwab offers Exchange Traded Funds (ETFs)		
		Schwab Bond Index Fund		
7	%	Schwab Total Bond Market Fund	SWLBX	0.29%

With State Street Global Advisors (SSgA) Stock Index Funds and ETFs

Item	Alloc.	Stock Index Fund	Symbol	Op.Exp. Ratio
1	%	SSgA S&P 500 Index Fund	SVSPX	0.167%
2	%	SPDR S&P MidCap 400	MDY	0.25%
3	%	SPDR S&P 600 SmallCap	SLY	0.24%
4	%	SPDR S&P World Ex US	GWL	0.34%
5	%	SPDR Barclays Long Term Corporate Bond	LWC	0.15%
6	%	SPDR Barclays Short Term Corporate Bond	SCPB	0.1245%

With T. Rowe Price Stock Index Funds and Bond Index Fund

Item	Alloc.	Stock Index Fund	Symbol	Op.Exp. Ratio
1	%	T. Rowe Price Equity Index 500 Fund	PREIX	0.28%
2	%	T. Rowe Price Total Equity Market Index Fund	POMIX	0.35%
3	%	T. Rowe Price Extended Equity Market Index Fund	PEXMX	0.45%
4	%	T. Rowe Price International Equity Index Fund	PIEQX	0.50%
5	%	T. Rowe Price US Bond Enhanced Index Fund	PBDIX	0.30%

With iShares by Blackrock Stock Index ETFs and Bond Index ETFs

Item	Alloc.	Stock Index Fund	Symbol	Op.Exp. Ratio
1	0%	iShares Core S&P 500 ETF	IVV	0.07%
2	%	iShares Core S&P MidCap ETF	IJH	0.15%
3	%	iShares Core S&P Small Cap ETF	IJR	0.17%
4	%	iShares Core MSCI EAFE ETF	EFA	0.34%
5	%	iShares iBoxx $ Investment Grade Corporate Bond ETF	LQD	0.15%
6	%	iShares iBoxx High Yield Corporate Bond ETF	HYG	0.50%

Three Categories – Aggressive, Moderate and Conservative using Model Portfolio 1 and 2 with Vanguard Stock Index and Bond Index Mutual Funds but allocation percentages slightly adjusted.

Risk Tolerance: Aggressive

Fund	Symbol	Allocation
S&P 500	VFIAX	25%
Midcap	VIMAX	20%
Smallcap	VSMAX	20%
International	VTIAX	25%
Intermediate Term Bond	VBIIX	5%
Short Term Bond	VBISX	5%

Risk Tolerance: Moderate

Fund	Symbol	Allocation
S&P 500	VFIAX	20%
Midcap	VIMAX	20%
Smallcap	VSMAX	15%
International	VTIAX	15%
Intermediate Term Bond	VBIIX	20%
Short Term Bond	VBISX	10%

Risk Tolerance: Conservative

Fund	Symbol	Allocation
S&P 500	VFIAX	20%
Midcap	VIMAX	10%
Smallcap	VSMAX	10%
International	VTIAX	10%
Intermediate Term Bond	VBIIX	30%
Short Term Bond	VBISX	20%

Your investments

Now that you have embarked on this exciting journey to financial independence list your investments below and keep track of their changing values.

STOCK INDEX MUTUAL FUNDS		
Name	Symbol	Value
1		
2		
3		
4		
5		
6		
7		

INDEX BOND MUTUAL FUNDS		
Name	Symbol	Value
1		
2		
3		
4		
5		
6		
7		

INDEX EXCHANGE TRADED FUNDS (ETFs)		
Name	Symbol	Value
1		
2		
3		
4		
5		
6		
7		

MONEY MARKET FUNDS		
Name	Symbol	Value
1		
2		
3		
4		
5		

Date:

TOTAL VALUE:

Tell us your success story.

Please send comments to:

The Riley Press1622 Payne Street,
Evanston, Illinois 60201

If you prefer, you can FAX to 215-243-7591
attn: Bill Riley

If you communicate with us, please include a daytime phone number and/or an email address. We will respond as soon as practical.

Thank you.